I0428589

A _VERY_ SIMPLE SOLUTION

Chemotherapy for a sick Uncle Sam

By

Richard L. Walton, C.P.M.

iii

Contents

Preface

Part One: *To understand where we are going, we must understand where we have been.*

Part Two: *Where we are.*

Part Three: *A Call to Action.*

Preface

While any number of "experts" and think tanks will line up to oppose the views expressed in this book, one must ask the question: Have *you* ever created a multi-million dollar balanced budget? The ideas and processes put forth by academics, politicians and financial "experts" have led us to the brink of disaster. The application of common sense and sound fiscal policy would be a welcome departure from the status quo: unending budget deficits and an out of control national debt.

If the same criteria were applied to economic advisors and/or Congress that applies to other disciplines (e.g. engineers, architects, etc.), the abject failure of economic policy and the spiraling debt would be no different than the failure of a bridge or a hotel balcony in Kansas City[1], and both civil and criminal prosecution would follow!

Does this solution require "outside the box" thinking? Well, it depends on whose box we are talking about. Literally thousands of local governments every year essentially practice the basics for the solution! Local governments cannot spend what they do not have, and there would be blood in the streets if your city or county went into debt to borrow money just to give it away. Former Congressman and speaker of the U.S. House of Representatives, Thomas "Tip" O'Neill, has often been

---

[1] On July 17, 1981, a walkway collapsed at the new Hyatt Regency Hotel in Kansas City, Missouri, killing 114 people and injuring 216 others. The Engineers lost their licenses, more than $140 million was awarded to the victims, but no one was found criminally liable.

quoted as saying: "All politics is local". If that is true, how is it that actions that the people would never allow at the local level are permitted, with abject apathy, at the federal level by their locally and regionally elected representatives? Clearly, the solution does NOT require outside the box thinking, and, in fact, such thinking has resulted in the debacle in Washington, D.C. All of the cautions and fiscal restraints contained in the local "box" have been discarded and replaced with unrealistic, crony-capitalistic, vote-buying, wasteful spending.

This country is poised for financial disaster. No one can deny the burden of the national debt, and yet we continue spending and increasing entitlements. A band-aide will not stop the bleeding of major trauma. Neither will half-hearted attempts to "control" spending pull us back from the abyss. The definition of insanity is to continue doing the same thing, expecting a different outcome. I offer a Simple Solution.

Richard L. Walton, C.P.M.

Part One

To understand where we are going, we must understand where we have been

Chapter One

A Glance at Budgeting History

Would you believe that **an annual federal budget**, as we have come to know it, **is not a Constitutional requirement**? The U. S. Constitution (Article 1, section 9, clause 7) states that "No money shall be drawn from the Treasury, but in Consequence of Appropriations made by Law; and a regular Statement and Account of Receipts and Expenditures of all public Money shall be published from *time to time*." (italics added)

At the time, men of character had pledged their life, liberty and sacred honor to their country. They would be appalled at today's practices of fiscal mismanagement.

One can only imagine how much worse things would be if Congress only had to account for its expenditures after-the-fact and then only "from time to time"! The first major change was the passage of the Budget and Accounting Act of 1921, which required the president to submit his budget request (for the entire federal government) to Congress for the following year. This Act also created the Bureau of the Budget, now called the Office of Management and Budget (OMB), as well as the General Accounting Office (GAO), whose name was changed to the General Accountability Office in 2004.

Prior to 1921, the structural evolution of the budget process was the development of the standing committee system. In the House, a temporary committee of Ways and Means was created in 1789, to advise the House on matters of Public Finance. The Senate took another 27 years before they established a parallel Committee on Finance.

Notwithstanding the War of 1812, the Federal Government, as a rule, didn't have many things to spend money on relative to the abundance of revenue being generated by tariffs and other taxes, so the lack of a formal budgeting process was of little concern.

Congress did, however, make an attempt to "control" Executive branch spending by authorizing and appropriating specific dollar amounts as opposed to the earlier practice of using the "…amount not to exceed…" language.

The distinction between a bill or law "authorizing" versus "appropriating" money had become a major issue by the 1830's. Simple appropriation bills were being bogged-down in days of debate due to the inclusion or addition of non-related authorizations and appropriations (now called "earmarks"). Former President John Quincy Adams, then a member of Congress, led the charge to modify the Rules of the House and the language was finally changed in 1837 disallowing non-related authorizations from general appropriation bills. The Senate passed a somewhat parallel rule in 1850, but it allowed exceptions, and, to this day, the Senate does not operate with a general prohibition against unauthorized appropriations. Basically, an appropriation cannot be made unless the spending was authorized by a *previous* bill or law.

[Obviously, the practice that the rules were supposed to have curtailed continues nearly unabated today. We have all witnessed Congress attaching unrelated and/or unpopular spending to a "must-pass" piece of legislation like continued funding for the Iraq and Afghanistan operations.]

As the country expanded its territory and number of states, the workload on Congress increased proportionally. By the end of the Civil War in 1865, the House established two new committees to share the ever-increasing pressure on Way and Means: Banking and Currency; and Appropriations. The Senate Finance Committee was similarly divided in 1867. It sounded like a good idea at the time, but Congress, as usual, created other committees with the authority to bring legislation to the floor without having to go through the Committee on Appropriations. Both Houses of Congress were guilty of letting things get out of control, and by the end of the century it was nearly impossible to keep track of all the various authorizations and appropriations. The problem was exacerbated by the Executive branch that was just as uncoordinated. Executive departments submitted their funding requests directly to the various committees with spending jurisdiction, sometimes duplicating requests to more than one committee.

Another piece of legislation, passed in 1870, came to be known as the "Anti-Deficiency Act". The intent of the Act was to prevent incurring obligations or spending money in excess of amounts available in appropriations or funds. It also prohibits the Federal Government from entering into contracts that are not "fully funded". While theoretically implementing the Article One controls of the Constitution, the Act went beyond stated power of Congress and included an exception where expenditures without appropriation were expressly permitted if Congress deemed

3

it necessary. It appears that Congress was expanding its powers less than 80 years into the Republic's existence!

[Although the Act, as amended, is current law, no one has ever been convicted or even indicted for violating its provisions in the past 140 years!]

In 1878, the Treasury Department made a valiant attempt to compile the various requests into a single "Book of Estimates". While this book helped with coordination and oversight, the President could not submit it to Congress, since there was no authority for a single budget proposal…nor was there any authority for Congress to consider one.

Throughout the 19th and early 20th century, the practice of budgeting was a "breathtaking" experience with only after-the-fact accounting!   It is almost inconceivable that, knowing the fear and dislike of debt that was expressed by Thomas Jefferson, Ben Franklin and others, some semblance of control of spending via strict budgeting was not made part of the Constitution.

Although obvious in hindsight, it wasn't until the Taft Administration that the idea of a regular process for federal budgeting was considered a worthy objective.   The President's Commission on Economy and Efficiency was created and, in 1910, published the "Suggested Outline for the Reclassification of Estimates of Government Expenditures on a Uniform Basis".   A draft of this document was submitted to department committees for criticism and suggestions.   Responses to this and to questionnaires sent to many foreign governments concerning their budget practices resulted in a comprehensive 564 page report entitled "The Need for a

National Budget". Included in this report was a message from the president. In my research on this subject, I have not found a more concise description of the problem and I am compelled to include it here, in its entirety, for its "shock-value". Nothing in our current history describes the out of control nature of our government's spending better than this contemporarily written document:

Warning: The following "*Message of the President*" may seem to be a cure for insomnia and may be difficult to read and understand. However, its historical value is too great to be summarily dismissed.

MESSAGE OF THE PRESIDENT

"Notwithstanding these specific Constitutional requirements there has been relatively little attention given to the working out of an adequate and systematic plan for considering expenditures and estimates for appropriations; for regularly stating these in such form that they may be considered in relation to questions of public policy; and for presenting to the Congress for their consideration each year, when requests are made for funds, any definite plan or proposal for which the administration may be held responsible.

Regular committees on expenditure have been established by the Congress for the purpose of obtaining knowledge of conditions through special investigations. During the last century over 100 special Congressional investigations have been authorized to obtain information which should have been regularly submitted, and much money as well as much time has been spent by the

Congress in its effort to obtain information about matters that should be laid before them as an open book; many statutes have been passed governing the manner in which reports of expenditures shall be made; specific rules have been laid down giving the manner in which estimates shall be submitted to the Congress and considered by it. From time to time special investigations have been made by heads of Executive departments. During the last century many such investigations have been carried on and much money has been spent in the conduct of these, as well as by the Congress for the purpose of obtaining facts as a basis for intelligent consideration of methods and procedure of doing business with a view to increasing economy and efficiency. From time to time Executive orders have been issued and reorganizations have taken place.

Generally speaking, however, the only conclusions which may be reached from all of this are that—

No regular or systematic means has been provided for the consideration of the detail and concrete problems of the Government.

A well-defined business or work program for the Government has not been evolved.

The reports of expenditures required by law are unsystematic, lack uniformity of classification, and are incapable of being summarized so as to give to the Congress, to the President, or to the people a picture of what has been done, and of cost in terms either of economy of purchase or efficiency of organization in obtaining results.

The summaries of expenditures required by law to be submitted by the Secretary of the Treasury, with estimates, not only do not provide the data necessary to the consideration of questions of policy, but they are not summarized and classified on the same basis as the estimates.

The report on revenues is not in any direct way related to the expenditures, except as the Secretary of the Treasury estimates a surplus or a deficiency and this estimate is based on accounts which do not accurately show expenditures or outstanding liabilities to be met.

Instead of the President being made responsible for estimates of expenditures, the heads of departments and establishments are made the ministerial agents of the Congress, the President being called on only to advise the Congress how, in his opinion, expenditures may be reduced or revenues may be increased in case estimated expenditures exceed estimated revenues.

The estimates do not raise for consideration questions which should be decided before appropriations are granted, nor does the form in which estimates are required by the Congress to be presented lay the foundation for the consideration of: Subjects of work to be done; the character of expenditures to be made; the best method of financing expenditures.

The present law governing the preparation and submission of estimates, requiring them to be submitted each year in the same form as the year before, was passed without due consideration as to what information should be laid before the Congress as a basis for action, the result being

7

that the unsystematic and confused method before in use was made continuous.

The rules of the Congress do not provide for the consideration of estimates in such manner that any Member of Congress, any committee, or either House of Congress as a whole may have at any one time the information needed for the effective consideration of a program of work done or to be done.

The committee organization is largely the result of historical development rather than of the consideration of present needs.

Inadequate provision is made for getting before each committee to which appropriations are referred all of the data necessary for the consideration of work to be done, organization provided for doing work, character of expenditures, or method of financing.

Following the method at present prescribed, the estimates submitted by each organization unit may have to be split up for consideration by appropriation committees of the Congress and be made the subject of several different bills; in few places are all of the estimates or appropriations asked for by a single organization unit brought together.

The estimates for appropriations requested for a single class of work are similarly divided, no provision being made for considering the amount asked for, the amount appropriated, or the amount spent for a single general class of governmental activity.

Generally speaking, the estimates for expenses (or cost of each definite class of services to be rendered) are not separately shown from estimates for capital outlays (or cost of land, buildings, equipment, and other properties acquired).

While the classification and summaries of estimates do indicate a proposed method of financing, these summaries do not show classes of work or the character of expenditures provided for and therefore can not lay the foundation for the consideration of methods of financing as a matter of governmental policy, as is contemplated under the Constitution.

The appropriations are just as unsystematic and incapable of classification and summary as the estimates—in fact, follow the same general form, making it difficult and in many cases impossible to determine what class of work has been authorized, how much may be spent for each class, or the character of expenditures to be made; nor does any one bill cover the total authorizations for any particular general class of work.

Bills for appropriations (the authorizations to incur liabilities and to spend) are not considered by the committee to which measures for raising revenues and borrowing money are referred, nor are revenues and borrowings considered by committees on appropriations in relation to the funds which will be available.

So long as the method at present prescribed obtains, neither the Congress nor the country can have laid before it a definite understandable program of business, or of governmental work to be financed; nor can it have a well-defined, clearly expressed financial program to be followed; nor can either the Congress or the Executive get before the country the proposals of each in such manner as to locate responsibility for plans submitted or for results.

Although the President has the power to install new and improved systems of accounts and to require that information be presented to him each year in such form that he and his Cabinet may intelligently consider proposals or estimates; although the President, under the Constitution, may submit to the Congress each year a definite well-considered budget, with a message calling attention to subjects of immediate importance, to do this without the cooperation of the Congress in the repeal of laws which would be conflicting and in the enactment of other laws which would place upon the heads of departments duties to be performed that would be in harmony with such procedure, would entail a large expenditure of public money in duplication of work.

The purpose of the report which is submitted is to suggest a method whereby the President, as the Constitutional head of the administration, may lay before the Congress, and the Congress may consider and act on, a definite business and financial program; to have the expenditures, appropriations, and estimates so classified and summarized that their broad significance may be readily understood; to provide each Member of Congress, as well as each citizen who is interested, with such data pertaining to each subject of interest that it may be considered in relation to each question of policy which should be gone into before an appropriation for expenditures is made; to have these general summaries supported by such detail information as is necessary to consider the economy and efficiency with which business has been transacted; in short, to suggest a plan whereby the President and the Congress may cooperate— the one in laying before the Congress and the country a clearly expressed administrative program to be acted on; the other in laying before the President a definite enactment to be acted on by him. (Italics added)

Included in this report are summaries of expenditures for the year 1911, summaries of appropriations for the fiscal year 1912, and summaries of estimates of appropriations for the fiscal year 1913. To these summaries your special attention is invited. Attached is also an appendix containing a digest of laws pertaining to appropriations and allotments, to the preparation of estimates, and to forms of reporting expenditures; also the suggested pro forma draft of budget, which has been prepared by the commission and is submitted for your consideration as a matter bearing very directly on the economy and efficiency with which the Government business is carried on."

Wm. H. Taft.
The WHITE HOUSE, *June 27, 1912*

The timing of this report could not have been worse, since 1912 was not just any election year…it was one of the most contentious presidential elections of the 20th Century! Congress did not have the fortitude to take on major legislation; the entire House was up for re-election; former President Theodore Roosevelt, who had hand-picked Taft as his successor, was throwing his hat back into the ring after an ideological split with him; there was no unified support for controlling the spending capabilities of Congress. There were five candidates running for president: Wilson (Democrat); Roosevelt (Progressive); Taft (Republican); Debs (Socialist); Chafin (Prohibition). Wilson won a lopsided victory with 435 electoral votes.

Congress did not consider a budget to be important until the enormous expenditures of World War 1 and the obvious inefficiencies of piece-meal appropriations. The House and Senate introduced a bill during the Wilson Administration that would require the president to prepare annual budgets for final disposition by Congress. Even though Wilson was a leading proponent of government reform, he vetoed the budget bill due to a provision that prevented the president from removing the comptroller, the chief government auditor, from office.

The 1920 election saw Republicans retake the White House and control in Congress. President Harding's campaign had touted a "return to normalcy", relative to the "Progressive Era" that had just ended. (In retrospect, it was just a pause.) That normalcy also included reducing the cost of government and increasing its efficiency. To that end, the president called a Special Session of Congress to consider, among other things, the passage of the budget bill. Finally, on June 10, 1921, the Budget and Accounting Act of 1921 was passed. The creation of the Bureau of the Budget (now the GAO) revolutionized government financing because it proved to be an effective check against the granting of money by Congress for purely political purposes.

The "forgotten" depression of 1920-21 was an extreme deflationary contraction of an economy reeling from the transition from wartime to peace. Instead of "fiscal stimulus" used by FDR in the 1930's and Obama in 2009, Harding cut the government's budget nearly in half between 1920 and 1922, slashed tax rates for all income groups and pursued a policy of laissez-faire toward "central planning" in general, and business, in particular. The Federal Reserve *did not* move to use its powers to affect the money supply and, by late summer of 1921, signs of recovery were already visible. By the end of fiscal 1922, there was a budget surplus and the massive national debt *was reduced by one-third*! By 1923, unemployment had been reduced from 11.7 to 2.4 percent (Lebergott, U.S. Bureau of Labor).

Having control of the federal budget and exercising constraints on spending led the way to the Roaring Twenties.

Even with all the spending and budget deficits generated by FDR's New Deal, there was no significant budget legislation until the Revenue Act of 1941, which created the Joint Committee on Reduction of Federal Expenditures. The committee tracked Congressional action vis-à-vis the President's budget request and issued scorekeeping reports to Congress while in session. The committee was replaced by the CBO in 1974.

Throughout the New Deal era and continuing through World War II, Congress's authority was eroded by the almost dictatorial practices of President Roosevelt. Congress had been complicit by delegating sweeping authority to the President to implement legislation as the Executive branch saw fit. The "emergency" posed by the war was the justification. The important checks and balances established by the Constitution were, in many cases, non-existent.

In an attempt to regain its legislative authority, the Legislative Reorganization Act of 1946 created the Joint Committee on the Legislative Budget. One of the key provisions of the bill was to reduce the number of standing committees. It accomplished that but, an unintended consequence was the proliferation of subcommittees. Since the bill allowed the various committees to upgrade staff to include experts on whatever was under consideration, the costs of the committees increased dramatically. Provisions required lobbyists to register with Congress and file periodic reports on their activities, but lobbyists quickly found loopholes in the legislation and avoided full compliance. The budget reform part of the bill dealing with budget deficits and the national debt could not be effectively reconciled, and, by 1949, no further attempts were made to comply with the bill. The Act was important because it was the most far-reaching organizational restructuring since the First Congress. Despite the Act's impressive accomplishments, as early as 1947, complaints surfaced concerning some of its deficiencies, loopholes, omissions, and failures. It took another 18 years before the general mood of Congress allowed consideration of another restructuring bill. Congress, with its usual speed, took five and one-half years to pass the Legislative Reorganization Act of 1970. For the first time in 24 years, and for only the second time in its entire history, Congress enacted an omnibus bill to improve its organization and operations. I suppose we should applaud Congress for trying to clean up its act but, while they concerned themselves with their internal rules and procedures, the budget deficits continued as well as a growing national debt. (The debt will be addressed in the next chapter.)

The Congressional Budget and Impoundment Control Act of 1974 includes a number of procedural changes and has been amended several times, including the Balanced Budget and Emergency Deficit Control Act of 1985; the Budget Enforcement Act of 1990; and the Balanced Budget Act of 1997. Budget Reconciliation Acts of 1985, 1986, and 1990 adopted what is known as the Byrd Rule (Section 313 of the Budget Act) in an effort to streamline debate and procedures on budget bills by not allowing "extraneous" items that do not directly affect revenue or spending to be part of the bill. A "sunset provision" is part of the amended bills. This requires a bill to include an expiration date if it is passed with just a simple majority. Otherwise, a bill must pass with a three-fifths majority to suspend the "Byrd Rule". The Economic Growth and Tax Relief Reconciliation Act of 2001 and the Jobs and Growth Tax Relief Reconciliation Act of 2003 are examples of bills that will expire at the end of 2010 due to the Byrd Rule. (A good summary of the Byrd Rule can be found at www.rules.house.gov/archives/byrd_rule.htm.)

It is a sad commentary that, after more than 220 years, Congress is, and has been, unable to exercise fiscal discipline. Nearly ninety years have passed since the first federal budget was authorized and, notwithstanding myriad "cost reduction" and balanced budget bills and amendments, deficits continue at an alarming rate of increase. Supplemental appropriations bills have been required to fund the Iraq and Afghanistan Wars. The Troubled Assets Relief Program (TARP) was passed in October of 2008. The American Recovery and Reinvestment Act of 2009 passed in February of 2009. The Healthcare Reform Bill passed in 2010. The "off-budget" spending and blatant disregard for the growth of the national debt should be seen as tyrannical, if not treasonous for destroying our country from within!

Government spending for the purpose of gaining votes and tenure is nothing new. It is a cancer whose growth began when this nation was in its infancy and has continued to its adulthood. This cancer can be cured with the "chemotherapy" of the Simple Solution I offer in this book. It can accomplish its eradication, but the initial side effects will require a will to survive that is only common to the American experience.

Chapter Two

Spending and the National Debt
(A very quick overview)

"There are lies, damned lies, and statistics."
-*Mark Twain*

There is nothing more misunderstood than that which we call the "National Debt". We constantly hear how we are "mortgaging our children and grandchildren's future", as if this were a new phenomenon. _Nothing_ could be further from the truth!

Alexander Hamilton called the national debt a "blessing", in the context of allowing a sovereign nation to go into debt to fund a war. Hamilton was truly a financial genius but, like the rest of our founding fathers, could not imagine the extent to which debt has been politicized and foolishly amassed.

With exception to a few months in 1835, when President Jackson paid down the National Debt to nearly zero, we have always had off-budget debt! As of January 1, 1791, after our first full year as a nation, the National Debt was a whopping $75,463,476.52! This was at a time when, for instance, a skilled carpenter earned less than 60 cents a day, and unskilled workers earned just a few "coppers" (pennies). Granted, this original debt was due to the Constitutional obligation to pay for debts incurred during the American Revolutionary War and under the Articles of Confederation.

Fraudulent Intent?

I'm sure that no member of Congress would *ever* acknowledge any intent to defraud the American public. However, as discussed in Chapter One, Congress has passed numerous bills to "balance the budget" but has failed to do so. A "balanced" budget in government-speak is not what it means in the private sector. It has been balanced at the expense of the Social Security Trust Fund, which, to no one's surprise, is not a "trust" fund by normal definition. How can a budget be balanced when it is well known in advance that "supplemental appropriations" (that add directly to the national debt and the budget deficit) will be required to fund the on-going wars? Congress is just going through the motions to "comply" with budget statutes. **In the private sector, they would join others in prison for fraudulent practices and "cooking the books"…Enron; Madoff, etc.**

War Debts

The only acceptable reason for any country to amass debt is to fund a defensive war. An individual can kill in self-defense, and a sovereign nation can go into debt in defense of its borders. Both cases create negative results. It was quite proper to honor the debts incurred by the Continental Congress and the Revolutionary War. Likewise, costs of the War of 1812 and the Civil War were justifiable.

The First Islamic War (Barbary Pirates)

As early as 1786, we started paying tribute, ransom and bribes to the various Barbary Coast countries in order to protect our merchant ships in the area. In winning the Revolutionary War, we lost the protection of Britain's massive naval fleet that had protected us from the Barbary Pirates. It was Secretary of State Thomas Jefferson that arranged the initial payments to Algiers, followed by payments to Tripoli and others not to attack our merchant ships. President Washington bemoaned the fact that we didn't have a navy to protect our shipping lanes, and a move was made to authorize the funding for building a navy. *The United States ended up paying $1 million dollars per year for fifteen years, as much as 20 percent of our total annual revenue!* The cessation of payments led to the threat of war, and, in 1801, one of President Jefferson's first concerns was fighting the war declared by Tripoli against the U.S. in May of 1801. The war lasted until 1805, and was followed by the Second Barbary War in 1815. Both wars were technically defensive, protecting ships flying the American flag, and the U.S. was the victor in both.

Mexican-American War

This was an *offensive* war, not *defensive*. It was the implementation of the idea of "manifest destiny" that was embraced by the population in general and most certainly by President Polk, who took office in 1845. No matter that this war was not defensive, it cost more than 13,000 U.S. lives and an estimated $100 million.

Disregarding President Washington's admonition against foreign entanglement, and as a result of full-blown yellow journalism exhibited by Hearst's and Pulitzer's newspapers, the U.S. was drawn into Cuba's fight for independence from Spain. Even though the Monroe Doctrine had exempted Spain's Cuban colony, the decades-long struggle for independence had deteriorated to the point of Spanish "concentration camps" and human rights abuses. Initially an opponent of intervention in Cuba, President McKinley eventually acquiesced to public and political pressure and supported our involvement in what became the Spanish-American War in 1898. This war added $250 million to our debt. A major side effect was our emergence as an international power, and one viewed as imperialistic by the rest of the world.

World War I

With full sympathy for all the lives and property lost and ruined, I cannot draw any other conclusion than that the "Great War" was an unnecessary tragedy of unwise treaties and alliances. The intrigues that existed both before and after the assassination of Archduke Ferdinand in 1914 are the 'stuff' of great novels. Sadly, those intrigues drew most of the world into World War I and led to events and conditions that spawned the next Great War. Although rationalized by many politicians at the time and since, the involvement of the United States was not defensive, but political. The price tag for our venture was another $22.6 billion added to the national debt.

Undeclared "Incursions"

U.S. Marines were present in Nicaragua in varying numbers from 1910 to 1933. We won't even go into the colorful 1850's, when the country actually had a president from the U.S. (William Walker), but he was executed in 1860. The civil unrest saw U.S. involvement in internal matters and siding with various characters both in and out of the Nicaraguan government. There is little wonder why so many Central Americans do not trust the United States. There is no total accounting for the cost of our involvement in Nicaragua, but we had thousands of Naval Personnel and Marines directly involved for nearly a quarter century. The guise was to prevent European intervention in the Western Hemisphere. We chased Sandino for years, but didn't get him. We did set up Somoza as a dictator for a couple of decades until he was assassinated in 1956. A familiar pattern in our history.

How about Haiti? We occupied Haiti from July 28, 1915, when 330 U.S. Marines landed at Port-au-Prince on the "authority" of President Woodrow Wilson to "protect American and foreign" interests. The last contingent of U.S. Marines left on August 15, 1934!

Representatives from the United States had veto power over all governmental decisions in Haiti, and Marine Corps commanders served as administrators in the various provinces. There was immediate opposition to the occupation, and in 1918, more than 2,000 Haitians were killed in a revolt. That was the same year that a "new" Constitution was approved by referendum, 98,225 to 768. The president had dissolved the legislature after they refused to approve the document, written by Assistant

Secretary of the Navy Franklin D. Roosevelt. This is another "ugly American" episode that explains much of the ill will towards the United States from Latin America and the Caribbean.

Why did Congress appropriate money for these and other incursions while we were experiencing recessions and depressions at home? Where was the oversight? Why was an assistant cabinet secretary writing another country's Constitution? So many questions, so few answers...

Word War II

This was yet another treaty-generated conflict. One of the Fourteen Points that President Wilson had taken with him to Paris to have included in the Treaty of Versailles was the establishment of Poland with access to the Baltic Sea and the port city of Danzig (now Gdansk). He got his way and a Polish Corridor was established that divided Germany from East Prussia and gave Poland the international city of Danzig, which had never been Polish and had a 95% German population. In early 1939, British Prime Minister Chamberlain, in an address to Parliament, advised them that he had given Poland assurance of British military support if Germany invaded. On September 1, 1939, Germany invaded Poland and 2 days later, Britain and France declared war on Germany...just about 25 years after the first "treaty" war of 1914 started. In December 1941, the United States entered the war after the Japanese attack on our Navy base at Pearl Harbor, Hawaii. This war eventually added between $288 and $338 billion dollars to our debt. The larger amount includes the $50 billion dollars worth of Lend-Lease debt.

The Korean War

This was a United Nations "police" action that saw the United States take the lead in expending men, equipment, and money. There were a total of 14 countries that supplied personnel in support of the South Koreans. This war was yet another result of third parties at the Potsdam Conference in 1945, unilaterally dividing a country without consulting the country involved. It became a "proxy war" between the Communist bloc and the United States and its allies. Our portion of the cost: $54 billion.

The Viet Nam War

Do we need any more examples of non-defensive political wars? There have been volumes written about this war, the reasoning, the strategy, the political damage and the effect on the American psyche, so I will not regurgitate the matter here. Suffice it to say, we added at least another $178 billion to our debt according to Defense Department estimates.

War on Terror

Not a conventional "defensive" war since we were not attacked by a sovereign nation. There is ongoing debate over the actions we took in the aftermath of 9/11, and I will not join that debate in this book. According to the Congressional Research Office, in a report dated September 28, 2009, the cumulative costs of Iraq and Afghanistan had reached $944 billion …and the number is still climbing.

Other Contributions to our National Debt

The "Old" New Deal

President Roosevelt's New Deal added between $32 and $50 billion dollars to the National Debt. It is difficult to quantify the actual debt figures since many New Deal programs still exist. Extrapolated cost on some of these, such as Social Security, Fannie Mae, The Tennessee Valley Authority and endless farm subsidies have been estimated to eventually be more than $50 trillion dollars!

The Marshall Plan

The United States' rebuilding of Western Europe after World War II had a price tag of $12.7 billion dollars.

Foreign Aid

Although Foreign Aid is normally a "budget" item, that is a moot point when, for example, The deficit for fiscal 2010 was $1.29 trillion dollars. Deficit spending increases the National Debt, so we are effectively borrowing money just to give it away. How's that working out for us?

According to the United States Agency for International Development, we are still supplying economic and military aid to more than 65 countries around the world. Maybe I've stumbled on the *real* meaning of "third world"; we seem to be giving aid to one-third of the world's countries! (There are about 195 member nations at the U.N.)

Buying our "friends" may be good for the State Department, but it is not good for the State of the Union.

As of July 2011, the National Debt is more than $14.5 trillion dollars, with total unfunded anticipated debt at more than $54 trillion. Interest alone is more than $1.9 trillion. Pay-as-you-go requirements are being ignored as we create the specter of another false emergency. We then can pass bills even though they will increase the debt under the guise of saving the nation from certain collapse. **It is now mathematically impossible to pay off the U.S. National Debt.**

No matter how "rosy" a projection, there has been no viable scenario presented that will enable the United States to pay off its long-term debt. The exponential growth in Medicare and Medicaid spending coupled with Social Security, as it now exists, as well as multiple antiquated programs that continue to be funded makes for a bleak future.

Ignorance or denial will not make the problem go away. I could write volumes about this subject, but, even with all the "spin" that could be mustered, the Federal Government itself is in total agreement! The 2009 Financial Report of the United States Government spells it out in detail with charts and graphs. This report, its summary and MD&A (Management Discussion and Analysis) can be found at the Treasury Department website and is a "must read" for anyone who has concerns about our future. A quote from one of the charts reads: ***"CURRENT TRENDS ARE NOT SUSTAINABLE BECAUSE PROGRAM OUTLAYS WOULD PERSISTENTLY EXCEED TOTAL RECEIPTS."*** Need I say more?

As bad as the 2009 Report is, the 2010 report will be measurably worse in showing how quickly we are speeding to the edge of the cliff. There is a solution…and it is simple.

Chapter Three

Money, Metals, and Manipulation
(Some interesting history, too)

Since the start of the Republic, Government has tried various methods of manipulating our economy. They tell us it is in the "public interest" and "for our own good". To put some perspective on where we are and how we got here, we have to bypass revisionist history and look at the facts as they were and the thinking (or lack of thinking) behind some important decisions. The common thread that ties all governments together is the unintended consequences and collateral damage resulting from seemingly benign decisions or actions.

Most of us would agree that when we studied American History, there was a predominance of information about our fight for independence and the creation and ratification of our Constitution and Bill of Rights. There is a perception that after ratification and the election of Washington as our first President there was a general 'sigh of relief' and, since the actual battles were over, an overall feeling of unity and resolve settled over the new nation. Nothing could be further from the truth. The Federalists and the anti-Federalists had disparate views over many issues that would form the basis and direction of our young republic. The Federalists had won the first battle by successfully replacing the Articles of Confederation with the Constitution. Some of the most important issues were the granting of Federal authority to levy taxes, to establish duties and regulate commerce between the states. The inability of the Federal Government to levy taxes was the root cause for the failure of the Continental Currency that had been issued to fund the Revolutionary War. The first issues guaranteed value by future taxation, while later issues really had no such assurance, and the future taxation and redemption of the currency never materialized. The value of a Continental Dollar, originally issued and accepted as equal to the Spanish Dollar, eventually sank to nearly 1000 Continentals to the Spanish Dollar. Between 1775 and 1779, $200 million dollars worth of currency was issued with nothing backing it up. The extreme devaluation prompted founding father John Adams to very concisely state the cause of the problem:

> "The amount of ordinary commerce, internal and external, of a country may be computed at a fixed sum. A certain sum of money is needed to circulate among the society in order to carry on their business. This precise sum is discoverable by calculation and reducible to certainty. You may emit paper or any other currency for this purpose until you reach this rule, and it will not depreciate. After you exceed this rule it will depreciate and no power or set of legislation hitherto invented can prevent it. In the case of paper, if you go on emitting forever, the whole mass will be worth no more than that was which emitted within the rule."

Had future generations heeded Adams' observation, many "panics" and depressions might have been avoided.

Although, even in retrospect, there probably was no better alternative to fund the war, the resulting collapse in commerce and confidence in the government gave impetus to Hamilton's desire for a stronger central government. Washington appointed Hamilton to be the first Secretary of the Treasury and he lobbied long and hard for a central bank and the establishment of a mint.

Conflict of Interest?

The Bank of the United States (BUS) was chartered for 20 years in early 1791 and opened its Philadelphia office in December of that year. As Congress debated the bank bill, Hamilton submitted his report on establishing a mint with a bimetallic (silver and gold, at a 15 to 1 ratio) standard. It took until 1792 for Congress to approve the mint and the first U.S. coinage.

Seventeen Ninety-Two ushered in the first financial "panic". The U.S. had issued $64.5 million dollars in bonds (securities) paying 6% interest in 1790, to fund the debt remaining from the Revolutionary War. When investors figured out that shares in the new Bank of the U.S. could be purchased, in part, with the government securities, prices skyrocketed, creating a bubble. As with all bubbles, it burst in 1791-92.[2]

Interestingly, Alexander Hamilton had founded the Bank of New York in 1784. In 1791, after communication with one of the directors of the Bank of New York, Hamilton convened a meeting with Jefferson and others to authorize

---

[2] Speculators had a field day since there were only three banks and more than fifty different currencies in circulation.

the sale of U.S. debt on the open market. The New York bank's purchases stabilized the price of the securities and effectively ruined the speculators that had created the bubble. The details of the manipulations would fill a book. Suffice it to say that Hamilton averted a devastating crash in the market and instilled confidence in the young country's financial condition. The behind-the-scenes dealing was obviously a conflict of interest but, as would happen in the future, the end justified the means and, with a positive outcome, was viewed as acceptable behavior.

I will reiterate that Hamilton called the national debt "a blessing", but that assumes the debt and spending is well managed and controlled. Jefferson, conversely, felt that any debt was a "burden on posterity" and was "a curse". History shows that both men were correct, but, for most of the last hundred years, Jefferson's case has been increasingly predominant.

Central Bank

Hamilton's unyielding position of the necessity for a central bank was, beyond doubt, the correct position for the time. As long as our money supply was backed by *specie*, which was the term meaning gold or silver, it had the full confidence of merchants, traders, foreign banks, and the general population. In an over-simplification, instruments of our national debt, such as Treasury Bonds, added to the "circulated" money supply since banks could, and did, issue paper money with the reserve backing of the treasury instruments it held. The Treasury Bonds were either implicitly or explicitly backed by gold or silver, thereby exuding the confidence of everyone.

Lest you think that it has been "smooth sailing" for the past two hundred plus years, consider this:

The Panic of 1792
The Panic of 1797
The Depression of 1807-1810
The Depression of 1815-1821
The Panic of 1819
The Panic of 1825
The Panic of 1837
The Depression of 1837-1844
The Panic of 1856
The Panic of 1873
The Depression of 1873-1879
The Panic of 1893
The Panic of 1907
The Panic of 1929
The Depression of 1930-40

Accompanying many of the Panics and Depressions were recessions:
Recession of 1802-1804
Recession of 1812
Recession of 1822-1823
Recession of 1825-1826
Recession of 1828-1829
Recession of 1833-1834
Recession of 1845-1846
Recession of 1847-1848
Recession of 1853-1854
Recession of 1860-1861
Recession of 1865-1867
Recession of 1869-1870
Recession of 1882-1885
Recession of 1887-1888

Recession of 1890-1891
Recession of 1899-1900
Recession of 1902-1904
Recession of 1913-1914
Recession of 1918-1919
Recession of 1923-1924
Recession of 1926-1927
Recession of 1945
Recession of 1949
Recession of 1953
Recession of 1958
Recession of 1960-1961
Recession of 1969-1970
Recession of 1973-1975
Recession of 1980
Recession of 1981-1982
Recession of 1990-1991
Recession of 2001
Recession of 2007-2009

While many of the economic problems in the United States were brought about by international trade and monetary policies, **our government single-handedly created the vast majority of our woes.** Although it seemed obvious, even at the time, that the Bank of the United States was a "good" thing, the Democratic-Republicans, Jefferson's anti-federalist party, still railed against it. When, in 1811, the renewal of the Bank's Charter was considered by Congress, it lost by one vote…the tie-breaking vote was cast by Vice President Clinton. The celebration was short-lived though. because without the control of the money supply both speculation and inflation increased. The War of 1812 created an extreme inflationary environment, and the government had trouble financing the war without the central bank. The credit and borrowing power of the U.S. had deteriorated to its lowest point since the founding of the country. As a result, in 1816 the Second Bank of the United States was chartered, also for 20 years. President Madison, an opponent of Hamilton's, was president during both bank charter fights and eventually saw the reasoning for a central bank.

Manipulation with Disastrous Results...The Perfect Storm

Earlier Panics were nothing compared to the Panic of 1819. The cost of the War of 1812, mostly borne by Americans, was a relatively minor issue that was being dealt with by expanding the money supply and repaying the debt with inflated dollars. The unanticipated peace between Great Britain and France saw a decline of nearly 80 percent in manufacturing and agricultural exports in 1817 compared to 1816. The United States had supplied both countries during the Napoleonic Wars and was not prepared for the peace-time economy. Retiring the debt from the Louisiana Purchase, primarily held by foreigners who would not accept anything but gold, caused the Bank of the United States to switch from an inflationary policy to a deflationary policy. The contraction of the money supply caused many state banks to fail and created a general panic in land speculation. In 1815, land purchases from the Federal Government totaled about 1 million acres per year. By 1819, the pace had accelerated to 3.5 million acres per year. This heightened activity gave birth to the axiom "doing a land office business". In order to "help" citizens buy land, the government allowed Americans to buy on credit. When the Bank of the United States, as well as state banks, began calling loans due and/or demanding payment in gold or silver, tens of thousands of borrowers defaulted…losing everything. Sadly, no one learned a lesson from this experience of attempting to "manage" the market.

Fast-forward to 1836. When Andrew Jackson ran for re-election in 1832, his primary campaign promise was to not renew the charter for the Second Bank of the United States. He was as ignorant or naïve about finances and the economy as he was brilliant as a strategist and military leader. Jackson believed that corruption and mis-management by the bank had led to the Panic of 1819. Easy credit and land speculation continued into the 1820's. Jackson saw this as "class" warfare: the common man vs. the elite of finance and banking. Jackson believed in "hard money", meaning gold and silver, and blamed the bank for all the nations' woes. In 1833, Jackson issued an Executive order preventing the deposit of federal funds in the Bank of the U.S. The funds were deposited in seven different state chartered banks. Jackson and his political rival, Henry Clay, used the Bank of the U.S. as their primary focus in the 1832 presidential campaign. With Jackson's victory, the demise of the bank was certain. Congress did not even send a charter extension bill to the president since they knew they could not over-ride his veto.

Although the U.S. was legally on a gold and silver standard, realistically, we were on a silver standard only. Gold was seen as more precious than the 15 to 1 ratio allowed for. In 1834, in yet another attempt to weaken the Bank of the U.S., Congress increased the value of gold by changing the ratio to 16 to 1. This move was favored by Jackson and effectively deflated the value of the bank notes issued that were backed by silver. Gold became the standard of exchange and silver was circulated mostly in small change. This was the first time that gold actually circulated.

Unintended Consequences

Between 1834 and 1836, land speculation increased five hundred percent due to all the "new" land that became available after "Indian Removal". The Government Land Office was only supposed to accept *specie* (gold or silver) or bank notes backed by silver, but, due to the volume of sales, bank notes issued by state chartered banks that were not backed by silver (soft money) had been accepted in ever increasing amounts. Jackson tried to get Congress to pass legislation to prevent *any* paper money acceptance, regardless of backing. Congress did not agree, so after its adjournment, and as his last official act, President Jackson, by Executive order, issued the "Specie Circular" which allowed only gold or silver to be accepted for land purchases. Most historians agree that this led to increased inflation and prices which created the Panic of 1837 and the Depression of 1837-44. President Martin Van Buren was blamed for the economic downturn, resulting in his one-term presidency.

The First Income Tax and Paper Money

There were numerous Panics, Recessions, and Depressions leading up to the Civil War. The enormous expense of the war resulted in the nation's first Income Tax. The government started printing money in massive amounts, and, to the government's surprise, banks stopped exchanging gold and silver for paper money. Once the banks ceased payments in specie, so did the Treasury Department. The income tax rates increased and so did the amount of money being printed. As usual, the government had misread the market and had no way of measuring the money supply. The initial issue of paper money was in the form of "Demand Notes" that were payable in coin at only a handful of banks. They were not popular and were discounted by many banks, which led to the termination of specie payment in December 1861. By February 1862, the Treasury received permission to issue "Legal Tender" notes. They were not accepted in payment of import duties or interest on the national debt.

At the time, Confederate notes and state bank notes were usually printed on just one side. The new Demand Notes and the Legal Tender Notes were printed on both sides with a distinctive green ink used on the reverse, giving them the name of "greenbacks", which has remained another name for paper money ever since. Sixty million dollars worth of Demand Notes were issued, while hundreds of millions of Legal Tender Notes were introduced into circulation. The United States did not redeem any paper money for gold or silver coin from 1862 to 1879.

In an effort to end the greenback debacle, legislation was enacted in 1873, 1874 and 1875, that had lasting effect. While grinding out the legislation, the Coinage Act of 1873, included a list of all coins to be minted. The Act included a heavier "Trade Dollar" for trade with Mexico and the Orient. In doing so, the standard silver dollar was omitted, effectively ending the bi-metallic standard in the United States. The Bland-Allison Act was passed in 1878, allowing the resumption of coinage of the silver dollar, most of which were not released for circulation but held in reserve to back the silver certificates. The Act did not establish a gold-silver ratio. The constant manipulation of gold and silver, as well as the money supply led to heightened inflation and recessions for the next two decades. There were more and more Acts passed by Congress in an effort to control monetary policy. Based on the number of Panics and Recessions, it did not work then, just as Congressional manipulation does not work now. Politicians have a bias against allowing the free market to absorb the changes in both international and domestic trade, as well as money supply. The presidential campaign of William Jennings Bryan in 1896 was based on reestablishing a 16 to 1 silver to gold ratio. His loss to William McKinley ended the organized support for a change in metals policy.

Bank failures and unrest continued after the turn of the century with more Panics and Recessions. During World War I, President Wilson embargoed the export of gold coins and bullion.

The Second Liberty Bond Act of 1917

Prior to the passage of this act, the Treasury Department had to go to Congress to receive authorization to issue debt (bonds and securities). This Act allowed Congress to set a debt limit, thereby allowing the Treasury Department to issue debt up to that limit without having to ask Congress. The First Bond Act of 1917 was an embarrassment to the government because the issue was under subscribed (they were not all sold), so a major campaign to tie bonds to patriotism was launched. The Second Bond Act basically established procedures that continue today with the Treasury Department conducting more than 200 sales of debt by auction every year.

Part of President Franklin Roosevelt's New Deal Legislation was the Agricultural Adjustment Act of 1933. This was the first "farm bill" of modern times and established a mechanism for farmers to be paid not to plant certain crops. Parts of this Act were found unconstitutional by the Supreme Court. The goal was to create inflation in farm prices to "help" the farmers. The Thomas Amendment to this bill authorized the president to, among other things, purchase the total domestic production of silver. The "silver lobby" wanted the president to "do something for silver". The purchase price for silver was established at 64 cents per ounce, while the market price was about 44 cents per ounce. Many historians agree that this drastic move to inflate the price of silver led to China (the only large country still on a silver standard) having to go off the silver standard and start issuing paper money. This created hyperinflation that helped destabilize the Nationalist Government and aided in the success of the Communist Revolution in 1948. The Silver Purchase Act of 1934 directed the Secretary of the Treasury to purchase silver at home and abroad until the market price reached 1.29 per ounce, or until the monetary value of silver held by the treasury reached one-third of the value of the gold stock. This Act also authorized the president to "nationalize" the silver industry. We had numerous international agreements that attempted to stabilize silver and gold prices but, as history shows, that did not work out too well either.

On April 5, 1933, President Roosevelt issued Executive Order Number 6102 requiring all persons to surrender all gold coin, gold bullion, and gold certificates by May 1, 1933. I encourage readers to examine the history of gold and silver manipulations of the 1930's. You will find that the "inside the beltway" thinking has been around for a long, long time.

The United States Defaults on Bond Payments

When President Roosevelt brought an end to gold ownership in the United States, a problem was created with the Fourth Liberty Bond Issue of 1918. The bonds, issued October 24, 1918, were callable starting on October 15, 1933, and matured on October 15, 1938. The problem was the terms of payment stated on the bonds:
"The principal and interest hereof are payable in United States gold coin of the present standard of value."

The Treasury refused to redeem the face value of the bond in gold since the President had made gold illegal to own. They based their refusal on House Joint Resolution 192 dated June 5, 1933, that essentially gave Congress the authority to change the rules after the game had started. There were 7 billion dollars worth of Bonds sold. Bond holders lost 2.866 billion dollars, or about 41 percent of the bond's principal. The Joint Resolution was found unconstitutional in Perry v. United States in 1935, but the court did not address damages.

The End of Gold

The Bretton Woods Conference in 1944 established the International Monetary Fund (IMF) and the World Bank. Exchange values of metals and currency were established between the attending countries as part of the United Nations. The Bretton Woods agreement required convertibility into gold for the United States *only* and only for external purposes. This essentially established the U.S. Dollar as the new international "gold standard". Twenty-five years later, after the continued foreign aid, free money practices of the Truman, Eisenhower, Kennedy and

Johnson administrations, exacerbated by the out of control inflation caused mostly by the Viet Nam War, President Nixon, unilaterally, without consulting the IMF or even his State Department, "closed the gold window" by refusing to honor the U.S. commitment under the International Monetary Fund agreement to sell gold to foreign central banks at $35 dollars an ounce.

Since late in 1971, and for the first time in the history of the world, every nation has depended on "fiat" currency: paper money with no gold or silver backing! There is no standard to which all currencies can be pegged. The fiat monetary system has been characterized by wide fluctuations in price levels, interest rates and exchange rates. As we have seen in Greece, Portugal, Spain, and Ireland, debt without hard reserves is causing international financial havoc. Unless the world goes on a program of extreme austerity, as many countries are now advocating (but not the U.S.), the outlook is less than rosy.

Part Two

Where we are

Certain truths *are* self-evident and the failure to acknowledge them will be our downfall.

Chapter Four

Social Programs

Social Security, Medicare, Healthcare

In this chapter, I will present a proposal that will *change everything,* with respect to Social Security, as we know it. I will not attempt to propose anything with respect to Medicare/Healthcare due to the passage of the Healthcare Reform Act of 2010. Many of the programs and changes will be phased in over the next few years, and the additional costs (or savings?) are unknown at this time. If a portion of the law is changed by future Congress', that, too, would have a drastic effect on costs. I *will,* however, factor in the cost of Medicare in the Simple Solution.

There is one major contrast between Social Security and Medicare: When retirement age is attained, benefits begin, but with Medicare, after paying into the system for all your working life, you *must* enroll when you reach 65 or you will be penalized for late enrollment. Then, unlike Social Security, you are required to pay a monthly premium (which is deducted from your Social Security benefit). The typical Part B premium is about $96.00 per month ($110.00 after 2010), but can be hundreds of dollars per month if you make more than $85,000.00 per year. To make matters worse, a supplemental insurance policy is purchased by most people to cover the items that Medicare doesn't. Average monthly cost of supplemental insurance is about $200.00. Do the math: A typical retiree pays at least $3600.00 per year for the "benefit"!

Nearly everyone has an opinion about our Social Security System. The program was controversial when first presented in 1935, and has remained so, to varying degrees, ever since. It has withstood multiple challenges that ended in Supreme Court Rulings. One could certainly argue that the very "general welfare" clause in the Constitution that was cited as the authority for the social program initially, could be equally construed as a reason to discontinue Social Security due to the negative effect of the massive debt on the "general welfare" of the "general" population. The program, like so many other federal creations, has been used, abused, and manipulated more times than almost any other. Its scope and benefits have gradually been increased, and will soon reach the breaking point (actually, the breaking point has been reached, just not acknowledged). Many of us can remember 1980; it doesn't seem that long ago. That was 30 years ago, and that same amount of time in the future, the year 2040, will be essentially "game over" for Social Security.

What would you think if you received something like this in the mail?

It's not an Entitlement, it's the

Social Security Sweepstakes!

Legal in all 50 States!
Automatic mandatory pre-registration at birth!
Payout for Life!
Citizenship NOT required!
Up to 92,480% return on "investment"! (Actual results*)
Must be at least 62 to enter Sweepstakes.
Sweepstakes payout begins when total benefits received exceeds total contributions (yours and your employer(s)) paid in.
Everyone's a winner. Even if you die, your survivors may receive winnings!
Sweepstakes ends when Congress acts responsibly.

*The first recipient of monthly payments from Social Security was Ida May Fuller. She retired in 1939, after having "contributed" a total of $24.75 in Social Security Taxes. Her first SS check was in the amount of $22.54. After cost of living increases and 35 years of receipts (she died in 1975 at the age of 100), the total paid to her by Social Security was a whopping $22,888.92, or a 92,480% return on her "contribution" of $24.75!

Although Ms. Fuller's case is an anomaly, it is a perfect example of why major changes must be made to the open-ended "give-away" entitlement we call Social Security. The unfunded liability is many *trillions* of dollars…with no end in sight…or even proposed!

The benefits paid to the average American retiree exceeds the amounts paid in by the worker and his/her employer in just a few short years, at which point Social Security becomes the equivalent of a Ponzi Scheme[3].

Every worker receives an annual Social Security Statement in the mail. This statement contains your earnings record and estimated benefits. The closer one is to full retirement age, the more accurate the estimates are, and if you total the amounts paid-in by you and your employer (shown on page 3 of the statement) and divide that by the estimated retirement benefit (shown on page 2), it isn't rocket science to figure out that in just a few short years (5 to 8 years for the average wage earner) the money is gone, including any earned interest. That is the *only* money you were entitled to…not one penny more!

The original plan was for no one to outlive the payout. It was flawed from the outset!

Is Social Security (OASDI): A fraud, a Ponzi Scheme, or stable retirement income?

Fraud: deceit, trickery, sharp practice, or breach of confidence, perpetrated for profit or to gain some unfair or dishonest advantage. No, not a fraud by strict definition.

Ponzi Scheme: Involves the payment of purported returns to existing investors from funds contributed by new

---

[3] "Ponzi Scheme" is named for Charles Ponzi and is used to describe any scam that pays returns to early investors from the investments of later investors. Ponzi's scam began in 1919 and lasted for less than a year.

investors. Kind of, after a certain point in benefit payments.

Stable Retirement Income: It depends on whom you believe!

Broken Promise

According to a 1936 pamphlet that may still be on the Social Security website, the Federal Government promised "…beginning in 1949, twelve years from now, you and your employer will each pay 3 cents on each dollar you earn, up to $3000 a year. *That is the most you will ever pay."* (Emphasis added) How's that working out for us?

When most of us think about Social Security, we think of a self-funded old age program that began in 1935. Reality is that the "Social Security" Act included multiple tax-funded welfare and entitlement programs.   Here is the actual caption to the Act:

> "An Act to provide for the general welfare by establishing a system of Federal old-age benefits, and by enabling the several states to make more adequate provision for aged persons, blind persons, dependent and crippled children, maternal and child welfare, public health, and the administration of their unemployment compensation laws;   to establish a Social Security Board; to raise revenue; and for other purposes."

In reading the Act, one quickly discerns that what we know as "Social Security" is only a part of the Act. It is also interesting that the employer tax was "front loaded" for employers of eight or more employees by adding an excise tax, too.

The tax-funded programs were ongoing, with future appropriations included in the law. Most of the programs were "grants" to the states, so long as the states' programs were administered under Federal guidelines. *The U.S. Social Security program is the largest government program in the world and the single greatest expenditure in the Federal Budget.*

One of the two Supreme Court cases affecting Social Security that were decided in 1937, shows the disingenuous nature of the government's position. In *Helvering v. Davis*, 301 U.S. 619 (1937) the program was upheld since "the proceeds of both [employee and employer] taxes are to be paid into the Treasury like internal revenue taxes generally, **and are not earmarked in any way**." In other words, this was just an exercise of Congress's general taxation powers. Just two short years later the Congress created the Social Security Trust Fund that certainly could be considered the ultimate earmark!

The other Supreme Court case: *Steward Machine Company v. Davis*, 301 U.S., 548 (1937) was a challenge to the legality of the Act itself. The Court, in a 5 to 4 decision, found that, *given the exigencies of the Great Depression*, it was allowable under the "general welfare" clause. Sounds like "Never let a 'crisis' go to waste." Revisionist Court: they allowed the situation to change the Constitution!

The Recession of 1937 was blamed on the Social Security "taxes" that had removed $2 billion dollars from the economy. Concerns over the complexity of the administration of the program added to the sentiment for the need for change. The 1939 Amendments to the Act made family protection a part of Social Security by increasing the funding for Aid to Dependent Children and raising eligibility age to 18. Wives, elderly widows, and dependent survivors of covered male workers were added to those who could receive old-age pensions instead of lump-sum payment upon the death of the worker. Additionally, the taxing provisions of the Social Security Act were removed and made part of the Internal Revenue Code, renamed the "Federal Insurance Contributions Act", or FICA. One can certainly surmise that this move was intended to thwart further court challenges. In the 1950's, previously exempted groups of workers were included in the program…and the "contribution" increased.

The "early" retirement age for men was lowered to 62 in 1961. I guess this makes sense within the beltway…as life expectancy increases, they lower the retirement age! Medicare and Medicaid were created in 1965, as part of President Johnson's "Great Society" Program. One important change initiated by the Johnson administration was the adoption of a "unified budget" which brought the trust funds into account, using the trust fund surplus to offset the total debt, making it *look* smaller.

In June 1972, Congress overwhelmingly approved a 20% increase in benefits. It also set up a cost-of-living adjustment (COLA) to automatically increase benefits if the Consumer Price Index (CPI) rose by 3% or more. Once again, Congress failed to meet even the lowest of expectations in approving a bill with a severe mathematical error in it. The COLA they approved actually caused benefits to increase at *twice the rate of inflation*! This was corrected later. The legislation increased benefits and established the infamous Supplemental Security Income (SSI), which is a welfare program not funded by the Social Security Trust Fund, but by the general fund. This program allows *immigrants who have never paid into the system* to become eligible for benefits when they reach age 65. The elderly and disabled poor are "entitled" to SSI regardless of work history. Helluva deal!

In 1977, President Carter signed legislation that increased the payroll tax to 6.2% of wages for employee and employer. With the increase in revenue generated by the new tax rate, the President remarked, "Now this legislation will guarantee that from 1980 to the year 2030, the Social Security funds will be sound." Well, that *really* wasn't the case: Social Security was in crisis within about 5 years! In 1982, it was estimated that Social Security would run out of funds by 1983! How's that for long-range planning?

The National Commission on Social Security Reform was empanelled in 1983, with Alan Greenspan as its chair. Their report brought about massive changes in Social Security by adding additional employees to the program, increasing the full benefit age, and making up to one-half of the Social Security benefit potentially taxable income. Even Congress and the president were made part of the program! Anything for additional money.

In 1990, all local and state employees not covered by a retirement program were also brought into Social Security. Just about everything that can be manipulated has been, and yet everyone acknowledges that "something" has to be done.

Congress has brought us to this point by the cowardly actions of adding to benefits in order to win votes. They did this repeatedly with the full knowledge that they will be out of office when the system collapses. Social Security has become one of the "third rail" issues that are supposedly "untouchable". There is only one thing to do.

Grabbing Hold of the "Third Rail"

Primary attention must be paid to one group of individuals: those workers who were required by Federal Law to "contribute" to Social Security. Notwithstanding all the beneficiaries that have been "tacked on" to the program over the decades, only those who have paid for it have a stake in it. For the sake of this example, I will divide the "payers" into three groups:
-Those who have already retired and are receiving benefits;
-Those who are nearing retirement age, i.e. 56 to 66 years old;
-All others, 55 years of age and under.

- On a selected date, ideally the end of a calendar year, all contributions to FICA by employers and employees ceases.
- The value of each worker's account will be determined by the Social Security Administration. Value will be all FICA contributions made by both the employee and employer on the employee's behalf since the employee first began work, plus the appropriate interest for the years involved, compounded annually.
- Each qualified worker (those with a SSA Account) age 55 and younger will be paid the full value of

their account[4] in one lump sum that is income tax-exempt.

- All workers age 56 years and older who are not receiving benefits, will be advised of the value of their account and will have the opportunity to exercise the one-time option of receiving the lump sum payment in full value of their account or opt to receive whatever level of benefit they have already accrued when full retirement age is reached. Because FICA contributions will have ceased, their retirement benefit will not increase, other than through COLA.
- Retirees currently receiving benefits will be advised of the value of their account and they will have the one-time option of receiving the full value of their account in one lump sum, income tax exempt. If they choose to continue receiving benefits, they will continue until the death of the retiree.
- All lump sum payments will be made from the Old Age and Survivors Insurance (OASI) Trust Fund.
- Actuarial projections will be made to determine the approximate funding required to pay benefits to retirees remaining in the program. Survivors must be factored into the projections.
- If it is determined that the OASI Trust Fund is not holding enough convertible securities to fund the projected costs, a Special Bond Issue will be authorized, similar to the Liberty Bonds Issues, to fund any anticipated shortfall in the Trust Fund.

---

[4] For the purpose of this example we will assume that an "account" actually exists. The accounting of the amount paid by worker and employer exists, but the money has already been spent on current retirees.

- The Disability Insurance (DI) Trust Fund will be evaluated for viability.

These actions would present some daunting issues: 1) Whether or not to continue the various welfare programs currently existing under the "Social Security" umbrella; 2) How to replace the "surplus" revenue that has been stolen and used to offset the federal budget; and 3) How to pay off everyone who elects payment in full.

The first issue would be to evaluate each program for effectiveness, efficiency, and necessity. Those who benefit from the programs will, of course, declare how necessary they are. The evaluation must be objective and if the program does not fill a genuine "general welfare" need, then it should be either phased out or summarily discontinued.

The second issue is one that will cease to be an issue due to reduced federal spending and a new tax structure.

The third issue will actually be fun to watch the free market at its best…without government control. Every worker will receive 6.2% more of their earnings. Every business will save the 6.2% add-on cost of each employee's wages; every sole-proprietorship will save 12.4%. These hundreds of billions of dollars will be available in the *private* sector! The additional billions of dollars entering the economy from the former government "IOU's" will respond like freed POW's, spending and investing at a feverish pace. This may sound hyper-inflationary but it should only create a short-term spike, which will level out by itself so long as the government stays on the sidelines and doesn't try to "fix the economy". The Simple Solution will cause a corresponding sharp contraction in government spending, so the net result will be neither inflationary nor deflationary. This is the ultimate "stimulus package". The vast majority of the newly available money will immediately be invested in annuities, IRA's, 401k's, etc. There will probably be new and innovative retirement accounts created by good old 'supply and demand'. It is not unreasonable to assume that many of the dollars will be invested in the very Treasury Bonds that will finance the payouts.

The act of solving the impending Social Security crisis will add stability and confidence in the U.S. Dollar. The debt sold to finance the IOU's and whatever additional cash may be required to pay off Social Security expenses will be finite, regardless of the number. The expansion of that portion of the National Debt will be eliminated…forever!

The Federal Government could also sell off some of its most abundant asset: land. The government owns more than 620 million acres, which is more than 26 percent of America. Land was once a major source of revenue; why not again?

An Absurd "Entitlement"

"I was forced to pay in, and, by God, I want my money!"

Let's say that, in lieu of FICA "contributions", you and your employer(s) deposited the equivalent amount of money in an interest bearing savings account or annuity. Upon retirement, you decided to use the same criteria used by the Social Security Administration in determining your monthly "benefit" that you would withdraw from your account. After working more than 45 years, you decide to retire at "full retirement age". You and your various employers have each deposited about $57,000.00 in your savings account. So, now you have, with interest, about $140,000.00 in your account. Based on the Social Security Benefits Formula you should receive about $1860.00 per month, or $22,320.00 per year. It isn't rocket science to figure out that in only about 6 years and 3 months the account is empty! On what planet would you expect your bank to keep sending you money even after you have zeroed-out the account? Would that be "Planet Ponzi"?

In 1950, each retiree's benefit was funded by 16 workers. In 2010, there are only 3.3 workers per retiree, and by 2025, there will be about 2 workers per retiree! In other words, in just a few short years each working married couple will have to fund Social Security Retirement benefits for ONE retiree! There is no way in hell that's going to work, and yet no one has guts to tackle the disaster we call "Social Security" in a meaningful way. I submit that my very simple solution is workable, possible, and necessary.

Just over 50 years ago, the nation mourned the death of the last Civil War veteran. That many years in the future will find us celebrating the passing of the last Social Security recipient! Wow! Now that's something to look forward to. The next item to consider is taxes…

Chapter Five

Income Taxes: Progressive; Flat; Fair; or VAT?

Before researching this chapter, I had only one bias: that our current system was an absolute disaster due to the Tax Code's enormous size and complexity. Beyond that, I had no "axe to grind" for or against any of the proposals that had been floating around for some time.

Our nation's first Income Tax was a flat tax of 3% on all yearly income above $800 dollars. The tax was passed in 1861 to help finance the Civil War. Within a few months, Congress did as Congress always does and started changing things: the income tax became Progressive, with the personal deduction reduced to $600 dollars and the 3% tax levied on income up to $10,000, and a 5% tax on all income greater than $10,000. At the same time a plethora of excise and "sin" taxes were established. The Income Tax was abolished (doesn't that sound great?) in 1872, and liquor and excise taxes represented more than 90% of federal revenue from 1868 to 1913. Another run at a flat income tax was made in 1894, but it was challenged and found unconstitutional in 1895. Its reason for failure was due to being a direct tax that was not apportioned to the states by population. The 16th Amendment, passed in 1913, allowed the taxation of income without regard to a state's population or apportionment.

The election of Woodrow Wilson in 1912 ushered in the most "progressive" era in our nation's history (until now). The new Income Tax (1913) affected less than 1% of taxpayers. The rates were from 1% to 7 % of taxable income. At this point, the spending increased at a greater rate than the newfound source of revenue. By 1916, the lowest rate was doubled to 2% and the top rate was 15% on taxable income of $1.5 million dollars. Rates were increased again in 1917, and massively increased in 1918: the bottom rate became 6% and the top rate 77%! Surprisingly, only 5% of the population paid income tax, meaning that the other 95% obviously did not! There is something fundamentally wrong with this picture.

Taxing the "rich" to benefit the "poor" was the net result of our progressive income tax, and has been the overarching philosophy since its implementation. One must ask if the number of "poor" have been reduced. Has this type of taxation helped our "poor" at all or has it created a permanent, growing, voting "unfortunate" class?

Redistribution of wealth or transfer of wealth is, by definition, a major trait of socialism, and many scholars and historians trace its beginnings to Karl Marx's *Communist Manifesto*, written in 1848. Sadly, there is evidence that none other than Adam Smith, the father of free market capitalism, had similar feelings when he wrote in the *Wealth of Nations* in 1776:

> "The necessaries of life occasion the great expense of the poor. They find it difficult to get food, and the greater part of their little

revenue is spent in getting it. The luxuries and vanities of life occasion the principal expenses of the rich, and a magnificent house embellishes and sets off to the best advantage all the other luxuries and vanities which they possess. A tax upon house-rents, therefore, would in general fall heaviest upon the rich; and in this sort of inequality there would not, perhaps, be anything very unreasonable. It is not very unreasonable that *the rich should contribute to the public expense, not only in proportion to the revenue, but something more than in that proportion."* (Emphasis added)

If one places Smith's comments in historical context, I think its relevance to today is quite diminished. Adam Smith lived in eighteenth century Scotland and England, where the monarchy thrived, as did the aristocracy, neither of whom worked. Taken out of context, the statement would most certainly seem to support Marx's writings, but Marx was writing about a very different economy than Smith. Nevertheless, it is obvious that any progressive tax scheme is, by design or result, redistributive and lacking in transparency. Contextually, it should be re-stated that what you subsidize increases and what you tax diminishes. Is it possible that Adam Smith wanted a stable aristocracy – so he advocated subsidizing the poor?

The lack of transparency of our current income tax system is both dangerous and destructive. It has made it possible for lobbyists to operate freely and undermine the well thought-out plans of our founders. Exemptions, subsidies and various other assistances are hidden in legislation that the legislators have neither read, nor understand. Because our tax code contains well over 67,000 pages and has been amended more than 16,000 times just since the sweeping 1986 changes, it is beyond "fixing"…it must be replaced. What could replace it?

Let's look at the "Flat Tax".

When researching the Flat Tax, I first read Steve Forbes' *Flat Tax Revolution.* Mr. Forbes has campaigned for president with the Flat Tax as one of, if not *the*, major issue and is one of its most vocal proponents. The Forbes Flat Tax is a single-rate federal income tax and corporate tax of 17 percent. Income is taxed once and only once. There are generous and refundable exemptions for adults and children. In an effort to keep anyone from paying more taxes than they currently do, the child tax credit is retained, as well as the infamous Earned Income Tax Credit (EITC). Taxes on savings, dividends and capital gains would be eliminated. The "death" tax (taxes on inheritance) and the Alternative Minimum Tax (AMT) are also eliminated.

Under the Corporate Flat Tax Plan, all profits would be taxed at the rate of 17 percent. Companies could expense all investments and there would be no depreciation schedules. Losses created by expensing the full value of investments in property and equipment could be carried forward. It is argued by some opponents of the flat tax that the elimination of depreciation schedules would recreate the real estate disaster of the 1980's. That would not be the case since real estate would not be a "favored" industry and would be on equal footing with all other endeavors. The Forbes Flat Tax would even be optional, allowing taxpayers to actually see the benefits of the flat tax over the current system.

There are a multitude of "Flat Tax" proposals floating about the internet and in book stores. Some would advocate a tax rate of 19 percent and not retain the earned income tax credit (EITC) or the AMT. There are many nuances to the various proposals but there appears to be one common theme: The major "Flat Tax' plans *do not* address payroll taxes (FICA and Medicare). Since Social Security and Medicare are the primary future debt issues, failure to deal with those issues while performing a major overhaul of the income tax would seem to be "much ado about nothing" or one step forward and two steps back. [5]

What about the "Fair Tax"?

Not having a foregone conclusion is a wonderful thing! When I first heard about the "Fair Tax", I thought to myself that it was not nearly as plausible as the "Flat Tax". I couldn't have been more wrong! The "Fair Tax" has been studied, maligned, shot at, and mischaracterized by just about everyone who has an agenda or a lobbyist in his or her pocket.

Men give birth…to an Idea!

In 1995, three men in Texas gave birth to the *idea* of a "Fair Tax". They assembled a group of non-politically motivated people to research "optimum reform" of our tax system. There were some high-powered individuals

---

[5] In addition to Mr. Forbes's book, The Heritage Foundation has a very good paper that answers many questions on the flat tax. It can be found at: *heritage.org/research/taxes/bg1866.cfm.* Included in this report are numerous references for those of you who wish to learn more about the subject.

involved and they were able to amass a 4.5 million dollar budget to fund the initial research and set a period of eighteen months to complete the research, introduce the solution to Congress, and get it passed into law. They found out rather quickly that they had accomplished stepping on just about everyone's toes. The introduction of logic and reason to the big spenders within the beltway is just about as alien as Congress following Generally Accepted Accounting Principles (GAAP), and being fiscally responsible. Nevertheless, by 1999, the Fair Tax Act was introduced in the House by representatives John Linder (R-Ga.) and Colin Peterson (D-Minn.). With each passing year, the bill has gained sponsors from both parties.

In 2005, Congressman Linder and Neal Boortz, host of the Neal Boortz Show, co-authored *The FairTax Book,* which became an immediate New York Times Bestseller. They followed this with *FairTax: The Truth*, in 2008, to "answer" the critics of the FairTax movement.

To date, more that $22 million dollars has been spent on research and analysis of the FairTax…much more than any other "tax reform". The FairTax proposal is so comprehensive that it includes abolishing all federal personal and corporate income taxes, gift, estate, capital gains, alternate minimum, Social Security, Medicare and self-employment taxes and replaces them with one simple, visible, federal retail sales tax administered primarily by existing state sales tax authorities. A positive collateral effect of the FairTax is how it will change the landscape for lobbyists: without an income tax, there will be no need to lobby for all the special "tax breaks" that are such a major part of the current tax code…sorry!

While there are some components of the FairTax that I have issues with, they are minor when compared to the numerous advantages of the change in our taxation. If I learned anything from my years in local government, it was that compromise is part of progress…and if the opponents to the FairTax used an open mind when considering the various issues within the proposal, and did their research, most would find a way to accept the FairTax for what it is: the most viable way to reform our taxes.

The FairTax Act (currently HR 25, S13) is nonpartisan legislation. The FairTax taxes us only on what we choose to spend on new goods or services, not on what we earn. The FairTax is a fair, efficient, transparent, and intelligent solution to the frustration and inequity of our current tax system.

The FairTax:
- Enables workers to keep their entire paychecks(no FICA, Medicare, or Federal Income Tax withheld)
- Enables retirees to keep their entire pensions
- Refunds in advance the tax on purchases of basic necessities (up to the poverty level)
- Allows American products to compete fairly
- Brings transparency and accountability to tax policy
- Ensures Social security and Medicare funding
- Closes all loopholes and brings fairness to taxation
- Abolishes the IRS
- Is revenue neutral
- Final price of goods would be about the same due to the elimination of imbedded taxes (imbedded at each step of the manufacturing process)

With the FairTax EVERYONE PAYS! Whether you are legal, illegal, a tourist, rich or poor, the FairTax is paid by every final purchaser of a good or service. There is no underground economy and no exploitation of anyone! We keep hearing we need to tax "the rich". This would tax the consumer – not the saver. The truly wealthy in this country are not taxed on income – they don't work. They are taxed on Capital gains, interest on investments…etc. They pay as little as a net rate of 15% in general. This is a truly fair tax – EVERYONE pays "their fair share" on what they consume. This should please the progressive movement since the rich tend to consume more than the poor.

The FairTax will both allow and require the nearly 50% of Americans that pay no income tax to finally pay "their fair share" of the cost of our republic. One could only hope that the passage of the FairTax would be the precursor to the elimination of all food stamps, housing assistance, aid to dependent families, etc.

Even those folks who pay no federal tax should relish the thought of receiving a check from the government each month in addition to the abolishment of the IRS!

Education before Legislation!

Because the FairTax is such a target for the opposition to demagogue, it is imperative that a major effort is undertaken to get the facts out to the public. The most misunderstood comparison is that of a consumption tax and the sales tax that most people pay. **The FairTax is not added to the cost of a new item** as sales tax is. The FairTax is already included in the sales price but is simply itemized on your receipt. Currently the various federal taxes are already included in the price of everything...you just don't see them.

I would be doing a disservice to Neal Boortz and Congressman John Linder if I tried to paraphrase the detailed information in their "FairTax: The Truth" book. As stated earlier, I highly recommend that everyone who is interested in saving our Republic read the book. Additionally, there is a complete library of information available at the fairtax.org website.

What about the VAT (Value Added Tax)?

A VAT is similar to a national retail sales tax but is collected at *every stage* of business production until its entire burden ultimately falls on the final consumer. Unless the Sixteenth Amendment is repealed before a VAT is implemented, taxes will become out of control in a very insidious way. Value Added Taxes are a stealthy way to increase the tax rate in small increments without incurring the ire of the population in general.

Proponents of the VAT argue that its imposition on top of the existing income tax would be an "easy fix" to the deficit because it would be difficult to evade (relative to the income tax). The evidence from many European Nations seems to show that the incidence of fraud in an effort to evade the VAT is widespread. There have been revenue shortfalls of up to 30 percent of potential tax collections in some EU countries...attributed to fraud. Europeans regularly raise their VAT's without resolving their debts. Our politicians cannot be trusted with this "new" source of revenue. We would end up paying more...for more of the same.

A Value Added Tax, in theory, seems to be a pretty slick idea but, in practice, is rife with problems. There are some great research papers available at www.heritage.org and they are worth reading if you are looking for factual information.

It is of utmost importance that all options are considered with an open mind!

Now let's consider a possible solution…

Part Three

A Call to Action

Make 2012 the Vote Heard 'Round the World!

Chapter Six

A Very Simple Solution: Chemotherapy for a Sick Uncle Sam

The Solution I propose is truly simple, but simple does not mean easy. The budget part may seem radical to politicians at the Federal level but it should be very familiar to most local and state government officials as well as every household in America!

The Very Simple Solution contains only *four* elements:

1) Phase-out of Social Security (as outlined in Chapter 4)
2) Repeal the 16th Amendment / Implement the FairTax (Chapter 5)
3) Pass a Balanced Budget Amendment
4) Budget by percentage of available revenue (this Chapter)

Most state and county budgets, and all Municipal budgets, are required by law to be balanced. Most City Councils, Commissions, and Boards of Supervisors are kept apprised of their government's finances on a monthly, or sometimes, a biweekly basis. Being aware of revenue shortfalls or cost overruns in nearly real-time allows budget adjustments or amendments to be made as required, thereby maintaining both fiscal and legal responsibility (just like you do with your finances).

The present Congress would not, in their scariest nightmares, consider what I am proposing, but…Congress is changing…the more, the better! Local politicians cannot, as a rule, get by with the uncontrolled spending of their Washington, D.C. counterparts (notwithstanding Bell and Vernon, California). All you have to do is apply the same logic and common sense to the Federal Budget that you do to your personal budget or your city or county's budget: you cannot spend more than you receive…kind of a no-brainer.

The present Federal Budget is projected to generate an additional $1.5 trillion dollar deficit! Wait a minute…do you have any idea how much a TRILLION is? A million seconds is 12 days; a billion seconds is 31 years; a trillion seconds is 31,688 years! A number that large is truly beyond comprehension, which plays into Congress' game plan: the less people understand, the easier they have it.

As if budget deficits aren't bad enough, what about the National Debt? Who in Washington has a plan for repaying the debt? No one has the guts to address it because, under our current tax system and spending practices, there is no way to reduce the debt.

In the real world, people would be thrown in jail if they kept books the way the federal government does! It is imperative that there be NO "off-budget" expenditures! Congress and the Executive Branch have played this shell-game for decades and it makes the entire budget process a farce.

How about a balanced budget?

How tough can it be?

There will be a lot of short-term pain and long-term prosperity. Here is the way it works:

I was originally going to use the 2009 Federal Budget as an example but, on January 25, 2011, the House passed H.R. 38, which reduces all non-security federal spending to 2008 levels or lower. The Resolution passed by a vote of 256-165. To remain consistent with this piece of legislation, the 2008 Federal Budget will be used in the following scenarios. (If there is too much resistance to using any particular fiscal budget, a ten-year average could be used to "smooth out" any anomalies.)

It must be stressed that, unlike the myth that Washington bureaucrats promote, there is nothing mysterious about the Federal Budget. There are more similarities with state, county, local government or your household budget than there are differences. The many comparisons expressed as a percentage of GDP (Gross Domestic Product) when discussing the budget, the deficit, or the national debt do more to confuse or confound the average citizen than inform them. Americans do not have a frame-of-reference with respect to GDP, but we *do* have a frame-of-reference when trying to balance money coming in with money going out.

I guess the mystical part is that the federal government can spend more money than it has...year after year. We know it doesn't work that way at home, so there must be something about the budget that we just don't understand. WRONG!!!

One must examine the culture that allows spending and unending debt. Notwithstanding the national debt that grew so massively due to World War 2 and the cost of the Marshall Plan, the general population was very frugal. American Express, Diner's Club and Carte Blanche were the only credit cards available in the 1950's, but they were used primarily by businesspeople and had to be paid in full each month. Folks actually paid CASH for nearly everything! Large department stores had their internal revolving charge accounts as well as lay-away programs. Cars, homes and major appliances were just about the only thing that were acceptable reasons for debt. Then, in the 1960's, came the onslaught of unsolicited Bankamericards and Mastercharge cards in the mail. OMG, this was like manna from heaven! Suddenly the discipline of not buying something you couldn't afford was gone. People were no longer limited to buying only what they could afford...they could buy what they w*anted*! It may be beyond the comprehension of younger readers, but by the mid-1960's, Chevy's and Fords actually had built-in air conditioning! Color TV's were all the rage. Historians concentrate on the civil rights struggle, the expanding Viet Nam War, the "Summer of Love", assassinations and riots...and for good reason: these were important aspects of the 1960's. Consistently overlooked or under-reported is the awakening of the buy now, pay later, credit/debt monster. This was the turning-point that made living beyond your means acceptable...and common. It didn't take too long before it became obvious that there was a limit to one's credit...and the bill had to be paid. Folks soon discovered that just paying the minimum amount due did not seem to reduce the balance...the minimum payment just covered the interest and not much more. *More than the minimum has to be paid or the debt will never be reduced!* Now, let's apply this bit of reality to the national debt. We will frame it as:

A Case For Percentage Budgeting

The non-discretionary (mandatory) spending in the U.S. Budget includes entitlements (Social Security/Medicare, etc) and interest on the national debt. If Representative Ryan's plan, or a version of it, were adopted, there would be a decrease in the non-discretionary spending for Medicare. Nowhere in the budget will you find any discussion, methodology, or even desire to reduce the actual debt. Percentage budgeting will allow for the actual *reduction* of the principal balance of the debt by attacking the discretionary (non-mandatory) portion of the budget, while at the same time creating a balanced budget!

It is important that we stop trying to fool ourselves. Passing an unbalanced budget is bad enough, but to then pass "special appropriations" to fund the Iraq and Afghanistan incursions and call them "off-budget" is tantamount to treason! Anyone involved with the unbridled increase in spending or the ridiculous QE2[6] (Quantitative Easing 2) perpetrated by the Federal Reserve should be arrested by the Secret Service. For those of you who think that the Secret Service is nothing but Presidential bodyguards, think again: Their original and still primary purpose is to "...safeguard the nation's financial infrastructure and payment systems to preserve the integrity of the economy..." It would not be a stretch to consider the creation of debt that we can't pay or monetizing U.S.

---

[6] Quantitative Easing 2 was another foolhardy attempt at stimulating the economy by monetizing U.S. debt through the purchase of Treasury Bonds with newly printed or created money. This action debased our already troubled dollar and can trigger increased inflation.

debt as tyrannical internal assaults on our monetary system. Back to the budget.

Picture the federal budget as a very large pie (flavor optional). The size of the pie is not nearly as important as the size of the various slices, each slice representing a department or agency of the government. Once again, I must emphasize that we are dealing with the discretionary portion of the budget. To put things in perspective, the 2008 Budget contained $1.788 trillion in Mandatory spending and $1.114 trillion in Discretionary spending. If I may state the obvious, $1.114 trillion dollars equals $1,114 billions of dollars (one thousand, one hundred and fourteen billion dollars). The budgeted revenue for 2008 was $2.66 trillion. Subtracting the Mandatory spending from the projected revenue: $2.66 trillion minus $1.788 trillion gives you a remainder of $872 billion.

I am starting a new paragraph here in an attempt to prevent your eyes from glazing over. Suffice it to say that the first part of the constant is:

Projected Revenue – (minus) Mandatory spending = Discretionary Revenue

Using the 2008 example, the $872 billion is the "Discretionary Revenue". Quite obviously this number is much less than the budgeted $1.114 trillion (1,114 billion).

The next step is to divide the Discretionary Revenue by the budgeted Discretionary Spending: 872 divided by 1114 which gives you 0.782 or 78% (rounded down)
So the second element of the constant is:

Discretionary Revenue ÷ Budgeted Discretionary Spending = Available Revenue

This means that you only have 78% of what was budgeted available to spend or in other words a reduction of 22%. This is the amount that would have to be shaved off each piece of the pie to actually *balance the budget!*

Twenty-two percent may sound like a lot, but in some line item's, budgeted spending increased by that much and more over the 2007 amounts: Global War on Terror increased by 45.8%; Department of State and Other International Programs up 22%.

Could this be done in just one year? Mathematically, yes, but politically, with only one house of Congress with numerous conservatives, probably not. How about accomplishing this in three years? Slightly more than 7% reduction for three consecutive years could achieve a balanced budget. This would be a much more politically acceptable method...especially when the normal attrition rate of federal agencies is factored in. The following is a breakdown of the 2008 budget by department/category.

- $481.4 billion – Department of Defense
- $145.2 billion - Global War on Terror
- $69.3 billion - Department of Health and Human Services
- $56.0 billion - Department of Education
- $39.4 billion - Department of Veterans Affairs
- $35.2 billion - Department of Housing and Urban Development
- $35.0 billion - State and Other International Programs
- $34.3 billion - Department of Homeland Security
- $24.3 billion - Department of Energy
- $20.2 billion - Department of Agriculture
- $20.2 billion - Department of Justice
- $17.3 billion - National Aeronautics and Space Administration
- $12.1 billion - Department of Transportation
- $12.1 billion - Department of the Treasury
- $10.6 billion - Department of the Interior
- $10.6 billion - Department of Labor
- $51.8 billion - Social Security Administration/EPA/Various Departments
- $39.0 billion - Other Off-budget Discretionary Spending

It is important to note that I am talking about percentage of *budget*...not GDP. So many numbers are either based on, or referenced to, Gross Domestic Product, and they cease to have meaning to the average person. Politicians love GDP for that very reason. One of the major components of GDP is "Government consumption expenditures and gross investment", which includes both National Defense and non-defense spending plus state and local government spending. Quite obviously, the timing of certain weapons systems purchases or aircraft orders can be manipulated to fall in or out of a given quarter having whatever effect is desired. Of course, I'm not accusing any of our bureaucrats of doing anything of the sort...

Pretty Simple, isn't it? But wait, there's more...

A Government Accountability Office report issued in early 2011, shows a potential savings of at least $100 billion by eliminating the plethora of programs that are duplicated in various agencies and departments. Applying the saved money to debt reduction would be a great start!

This is actually something that *can be done!* This is where a close examination of the *need* for certain departments takes place.

Senator Rand Paul (R-KY) recently unveiled his 5-year budget plan that eliminates four agencies: Education; Energy; Commerce; and Housing and Urban Development. If just these four agencies were eliminated (Education, Energy, Commerce, HUD), about $116 billion could be cut, thereby reducing the budgeted discretionary amount from $1114 billion to about $998 billion. Now the $872 billion can be divided by the reduced budgeted amount of $998 billion to determine the percentage of reduction required to operate within revenue constraints. The new number would be a 12.7 % reduction across the board! You will see how this can be achieved in Chapter Seven.

Take the Department of Education...please! The nation got by just fine for the first 200 years without a cabinet level department, but in 1979, President Carter signed it into existence during his last year in office. Its 1980 budget was $14 billion dollars. The amount in the 2011 budget is about $82 Billion! The United States historically had a decentralized educational scheme. Local and state governments used to be in charge. School taxes are still some of the highest taxes paid by homeowners. The more our federal government has gotten involved with education, the worse the outcome. President Reagan couldn't eliminate the department, although it had been a campaign issue. His Democrat-controlled Congress would not go for it. Many scholars and politicians have made the case that the Constitution does not give the federal government any power with respect to education...that power was reserved for the states. The Department of Education would be the most logical to do away with.

The Energy department was created to develop and maintain our energy resources and provide us with energy independence. How's that working for us. It is a department that does not work, cannot accomplish what it was set up to do and should be abolished.

The Commerce department, instead of assisting us with commerce, has become an obstacle to commerce. It needs to go – so the free market can, once again, flourish in our country.

All we need to do is look at the results of HUD to know it was a well intentioned but misguided effort to develop our urban areas. It is another example of government inefficiency. The private sector of our economy could provide all the services HUD tries to do and they would do it better.

Senator Rand Paul is right. We need to reallocate our resources to more important projects – like paying off the national debt.

Chapter Seven

Cutting to the Chase

A politically acceptable application of the Very Simple Solution

Since magic wands are hard to come by, a rational, logical approach must be utilized in applying the Simple Solution. Absent a fiscally conservative Congress and President, the highest priority must be to see that ultra-conservatives achieve decisive majorities in both houses of Congress *and* win the White House in 2012.

Taking the four elements of the Simple Solution (Phase-out of Social Security, as outlined in Chapter 4; Repeal the 16th Amendment / Implement the FairTax in Chapter 5; Pass a Balanced Budget Amendment; Budget by percentage of available revenue, outlined in Chapter 6) in reverse order is the most likely to achieve results.

Using the 2008 budget amounts would require a 12.7 % (assuming the elimination of the Departments of Education; Energy; Commerce, and HUD) across-the-board reduction in Discretionary Spending. Obviously, attempting this large of reduction in one fell swoop would be difficult to get through Congress, but a 6.5 % reduction per year for two consecutive years *is* possible. While even a 6.5 % reduction may seem draconian, it really isn't: the average annual attrition rate for federal employees is somewhere between 5.8 and 9.4 percent, depending on who is publishing the numbers. According to a Partnership in

Public Service report, some agencies have two-year attrition rates *exceeding 35 percent*! (Treasury, Commerce and Homeland Security) Making use of attrition would soften the impact to an acceptable...and politically viable level. Private sector reductions-in-force are oftentimes much greater than what is being suggested.

While percentage budgeting is being implemented, the push for a balanced budget amendment could reasonably get off to a good start.

The implementation of the FairTax and the repeal of the 16th Amendment would probably have to wait until after the 2012 election due to the make-up of the Congress and Administration. Likewise, the phasing-out of Social Security will require a super-majority of conservatives in Congress with the intestinal fortitude to ward off the attacks from AARP and other lobbying groups.
Consider this *piece de resistance* of conservative planning:

If the scenario eliminating four agencies/departments were applied, instead of using the available $872 billion for discretionary spending, take $100 billion off the top and apply it to the *principal* of the national debt...not just interest payments! This would drastically reduce the available funds and cause further trimming of each department but...short-term pain for long-term gain. The amount of the required reduction would be about 22.7 %, or about 7.5% reduction for three years. A portion of the $100 billion could be set aside for domestic national emergencies such as hurricanes, floods, etc. The emergency funds would be untouchable for anything other than domestic emergencies! (not earthquakes in Haiti, for instance.)

Oh, this is called "shared sacrifice" - where the government also shares in the sacrifice!

This *is* possible to accomplish with a fiscally conservative Congress and Administration with the will to set a more Constitutional path to the future.

Grabbing hold of the "other" Third Rail

The "other" untouchable third rail is the Defense Department Budget. Many, if not most Conservatives won't even discuss cutting defense spending. Why? We have military bases in more than 60 countries around the world. We have a military or intelligence presence in more than 130 countries. We have around 50,000 military personnel permanently stationed in Germany. World War II and the Cold War are over! The Korean War was a United Nations effort, so why are *we* still there? The most heavily militarized border in the world is the DMZ between North and South Korea and two of the least militarized and most porous borders are to the north and south of the United States.

The North Atlantic Treaty Organization (NATO) was created as a defense pact against the former Soviet Union. With the fall of the Berlin Wall and the collapse of the Soviet Union, NATO's entire mission changed, but no one thought to re-examine the cost-benefit of the organization. The Bosnian War in 1993, the Kosovo War in 1999, and the incursion into Afghanistan in 2003, were all NATO operations. Of course, we can't forget the current Libyan fiasco.

Our civilian leadership have constantly deferred to the Pentagon and Department of State to evaluate and "justify" our international military/intelligence presence. I would submit that efficiency and budgetary considerations are not part of the game. There is no doubt that we can reduce our worldwide presence without negative effect on our national interests. The protection of our borders should, and must be, given the highest priority.

Chapter Eight

Random Thoughts

What is our Mission Statement?

Let's READ our Constitution! That fine document *is* this country's Mission Statement, and if we only adhered to the limitations placed on the central government by that document, it would not be difficult to "trim" the budget and set the course for fiscal responsibility!

Sadly, a very specific and confining Amendment to the Constitution requiring a balanced budget is the only hope for the future. Our history shows us that the creature we call Congress is genetically incapable of reigning in spending and living within its means.

Americans are the most generous people in the world. What makes the federal government think they can do a better job of providing for the needy than the local and state governments? We know when our neighbor is in need. We know when our neighbor is scamming the system. The federal government does not. They are a lot further from the problem and their sight is limited.

One needs to make the point that once, Americans prided themselves on self- reliance and our ability to stand on our own two feet. The current trend in government assistance has created a generation of people who whine about how unfair the system is – and want the system to feed them, house them, educate them, provide employment (a place to spend their day – not a job to do), and pay them retirement when they have completed their years of servitude to the system. We now denigrate the ones who have worked hard at any task that needed to be done, learned how to do something very well (so they may demand payment for that knowledge), and saved and amassed enough money to retire while raising their family. We are now talking about "means testing" for Social Security – once again, penalizing the ones who looked ahead and planned for the future. WHAT YOU SUBSIDIZE INCREASES! Stop with all the welfare programs that create this needy class of whiners – reward the ones who are willing to work and provide for themselves.

If our republic is truly a government of, by, and for the people, it is the duty of every citizen to be reasonably well informed with respect to current issues, the agendas of the progressives and liberals as well as the conservatives. People will say that they don't have the time or the desire to get involved and yet they can quote scenes of the Seinfeld show verbatim. The ratings for mindless TV comedies and reality shows are an indication that the reason people don't have the time is that they have squandered it on the irrelevant pop-culture of today.

I find it quite ironic that the no-drill progressives that decry our importation of foreign oil continue to wander around holding on to their plastic water bottles. Hello! Plastic is made from OIL!

Each time that Congress has extended unemployment benefits, the cost has added directly to expanding deficit and consequently the national debt.

Since the Supreme Court has found that Poll Taxes and Literacy Tests are unconstitutional, thereby allowing dumbass freeloaders the "right" to vote, there should be the implementation of a "Conflict of Interest" qualifier in both state and federal elections. Anyone who receives unearned "benefits" from the government (not Social Security or Medicare) should not be allowed to vote. In most all legislative and judicial proceedings, anyone with a conflict of interest must recuse themselves from deliberations or voting. Think about it!

If your elected representatives are not truly representing you, just withhold contributions to their campaign. If the RNC or DNC is off-track...don't donate! Sad to say, money talks louder than ideals at election or re-election time. Be sure to let them know why you are withholding support. It may make a difference if enough people act accordingly.

Conclusion

One of the greatest problems in Washington is the continuity of the bureaucracy. New members of the House and Senate come to Washington with great ideas and a desire for change. They select their new staff members and then they realize that they are all strangers in a strange land. There are no road maps or instruction manuals to guide them to their intended destination, a destination filled with cuts in spending and less government control. The dark desert highway has no guideposts or direction signs so, just as a traveler would do, you ask for directions at the lonely gas station or café. A typical traveler would graciously accept the directions and information from the old guy at the gas station or the helpful waitress at the cafe and be on their way with new confidence in their journey. This is essentially what happens in Washington, except that the gas station attendant and the helpful waitress are career bureaucrats, the vast majority of whom have never worked in the private sector and only know the ways of government largess. Career bureaucrats, for the most part, have never had to make a profit, meet a payroll, operate efficiently, or be held accountable for the success or failure of their department. The information and direction they give is probably sincere and well meaning, but if they only know the ways of government, their input will only perpetuate the status quo that is fraught with automatic budget increases and an ever-expanding federal presence in the lives of Americans.

Washington bureaucrats are the antithesis of their private sector counterparts. Their inability or unwillingness to operate efficiently or in a more cost effective manner is an issue of major concern. Electing the cost-cutters to Congress is just the first step in fundamental transformation that is absolutely essential. Close examination and evaluation of career bureaucrats should be the second step of the arduous journey.

Since the world has been operating with fiat currency since the early seventies, the "Keynesian Crowd" has had free reign to apply their central bank manipulation and government "stimulus" spending at will. How well has that worked out for anyone? If hard currency is such a foolhardy thing, why are so many countries buying all the gold they can acquire?

When we start discussing a global currency, we should be sure it is based on specie! A bi-metal standard of gold and silver would be a self regulating instrument.

Got Tea?